Before I Say Goodbye

Before I Say Goodbye

Janette Valenzo

Copyright © 2022 Before I Say Goodbye

All rights reserved. no part of this publication may be reproduced, distributed ut the prior written permission of the publisher, except in the case of brief quotations embodied in critical reviews and certain other noncommercial uses permitted by copyright law. For permission requests, write to the publisher, addressed "attention: Permissions Coordinator," at the e-mail address below.

davina@alegriamagazine.com

Editor and writer: Valenzo, Janette
1st Edition

ISBN: 978-1-7379927-8-3

Published by Alegria Publishing
Book cover by Alexandra Lenihan
Layout by Janette Valenzo, Lorraine Dean, & Krystle May Statler

To the hopeless romantic:

You are not too much.
You are not not enough.
You are perfect.

CONTENTS

Foreword   11
Preface   12
Prologue   14

Act I: The Beginning
Love Like this   16
Thirsty   17
Azul   18
Red Wine   19
Haunted   20
Can I Ask You Something?   21
There's a Secret Message in This One   23
Jupiter   24
The Answer   25
You Forgot Something   26
Unholy   28
Love Bombs   29
You Said You Didn't Want to be a Father   30
A Funeral of One   31

Act II: The Rising
The Kiss   34
Gaslighter   35
Adams   36
Would You Like a Refill?   37
The Twist Everyone Saw Coming   39
Every Love Story Needs a Fuck You Poem   40
My Hope in Your Sins   41
Did You Really Just Ask Me That?   42
Magdalena   43
Can I Ask You Something? *(Reprised)*   44
Character Development   45
In The Garden   46

Act III: The Climax
The Wind   50
Woman Like Me   51
Into the Flames   52
Orange   53

Maneater	54
The Hook Up After the Break Up	57
Upon Entering	58
I've Read This Somewhere Before	59
Skipping Ahead	61
The Ending is Here	62
Alternate	63
Before I Say Goodbye… Again	64

Act IV: The Fallout

Genre	66
Mothered	67
Our Games	68
Habits	69
Stay	70
An Insomniac's Prayer	71
Rain Room	72
The Final Death	73
The Night the Devil and I Never Met	74
Why God Made Women	75
Ritual	77

Act V: The End

And on the Third Day…	80
Daydreamer	81
Alarms	82
Peach Cobbler	83
For When They Try To Feed Bullshit	85
To Never Being Certain	86
Just a List of Things I Did	87
Today	88
Viole(n)t	89
What Will I Do When This Book is Done?	90
Bathroom Stall Lesson	91
When All Was Lost	93
A Love Only The Gods Can Hear	94
Private Paradise	99

Epilogue	100
Acknowledgments	103
About the Author	107

Foreword
By Tonya Ingram, Poet

"I dreamt of love for so long, I forgot what love looked like awake."

Janette Valenzo's *Before I Say Goodbye* is a tour of the heart: the beat, the break, the bloom. Recall a love that left you breathless and a love that demanded you take your breath back. That you return to the one who deserves your love the most: yourself.

This book is a love letter to our vulnerability. It is a declaration to anyone who held our bodies and not our names. It is to say I was here first.

Reader, if you wish to come home to you, this is the manual of feelings to call friend. Janette's gut-wrenching honesty reminds us that love is messy and miraculous. Each poem unfolds like prayer, carefully resurrected for those of us learning our worth. Divided into a five-course meal, *Before I Say Goodbye* honors the beginning, middle and end of what it means to show up in a relationship.

If there is new love in your life, this book is for you. If there are troubled waters in the ocean of your love, this book is for you. If you are landing into the softest parts of self-love, this book is for you.

It takes courage to love. To welcome another into the mansion of your heart and hope they know how to set the table or dry the dishes. To be in love with another is to be an open door. To be in love with yourself is to be the whole damn house.

Sometimes in love we say hello to what could be: the hours spent cuddling or marathoning anything on Netflix. But there are other times we must say goodbye to what was possible. We say goodbye to the names we did not deserve, the fights that lasted too long, the silences that made a home. We say goodbye to them so that we can welcome back ourselves. But before we go, we must leave a few words as testimony. *Before I Say Goodbye* is the curtain call, the last word, the gospel that brings us home.

Preface

This is a love story.
>If you are a hopeless romantic, this book is for you. If you aren't, this book is still for you.

This love story begins like most modern love stories usually do:
>Girl meets Boy at a bar. Girl asks Boy out. Girl falls in love.

When I started this love story, the whole premise was about falling in love *and* staying in love. It was beautiful, and then it wasn't.

My therapist once shared that it takes 6 months to a year to really know someone. Until then, you are dating the potential you have projected onto them, or whoever they are pretending to be.

So when this love story came crashing down, this book took a different direction. Bright side: I have enough poems for a trilogy!

But back to this book.
>Like most love stories, Boy comes back. Girl really hopes for the best, but she is no longer a girl. She has grown and he has not.

This is still a love story.
>Just not the story I had hoped for, but the love I needed.

This is still a love story,
>but one where Girl needs to walk away. Not because she doesn't love Boy. She does. In fact, so much that she would have written a whole library for Boy, but love is not enough.

This is a love story
>for those who believe if they can love a bit more,
>they can change the story.

You can change the story.
>You just need to change the love interest.
>That new and forever love interest is you.

… Before I Say Goodbye

Prologue

if a tree falls in a forest
philosophical questions are asked

if i fall in love
i break every bone in my body
no sound but the echo lasts

Act I: The Beginning

Love Like This

When I love you,
do not thank me.
Instead,
    compose a thousand love letters in poetry and academia,
      capturing the feeling of every cell in your body
          yearning to hold mine.
        Wrap my nerves in starlight,
      and trace constellations down my back,
       as you kiss me and inhale my exhales,
     resuscitating you in ways oxygen never could.

When I wish to love you for a million lifetimes,
do not reply how that is nice of me now.
Instead,
    promise to love me a million times more in this one life.
      Each heartbeat more jealous of the last
    until they crash into each other like waves on a shore
      begging to know what it means to drown in love.

When I give you my heart,
keep yours.
Instead,
      Give me your appendix, your gallbladder,
     the parts of you that are not mentioned in public
      but you wonder what purpose they serve you.
         Serve them to me.
      I will devour them all on hand and knee.
          And after,
        if you consume me
    with a fervor that outstrikes a billion matches,
      and walk through the flames
       and into my arms,

I will know then you love me
as much as I love you.

Thirsty
First Published with Acid Verse: Queer Uprising January 2021

I inhaled drinks like water to quiet a thirst I would not name,
but each drop, a dehydration I could not stop.
I begged the blessed skies in California bars,
but acid poured instead from the ceilings,
as if God Herself was emptying the cup down my throat.

Or did it slip through Her fingers
as your hand brushed against mine?

My throat scorched
and you, a wildfire I could not look away from.

My cheeks, a blushing flame
matching the color of your smile.

My hands reaching out in prayer
as you refilled my unholy cup.

As the night progressed,
I tasted fire in the water
dripping from the tap
as this thirst possessed
every molecule of my hell-bent soul.

I prayed my God-fearing upbringing
could forgive this Devil-in-a-dress downfall,
but to Hell with past teachings
with you presently before me.

The angels would kill for the way you were bartending
to my needs.
Demons would repent at the sound of our glasses
clinking a hallowed toast.

We were
sober and drunk /
blessed and cursed.

Two thirsty souls in a California bar
with nothing but our hearts on our sleeves
and our names nowhere to be found.

Until you shared yours,
and my thirst finally had a name.

Azul

half timing, half luck
empty words, fully drunk
my heart was beating the blues

locked eyes, crossed signs
friends there, wasted times
your chest bathed in blue

games played, soulful bets
short shorts, longer legs
my blue heels walked over to you

two players, zero risk
wrong timing, what a miss
that summer apart was too blue

months later, one call
out of luck, first Fall
midnight black fell into blue

and I fell for you

Red Wine

Until you,
I was tea and white wine.
Lost every morning deciphering dried-up leaves in cracked mugs.
Trying to find myself at the bottom of drunk-down glasses
in the evenings.

No more time for
red wine and indigo lips,
frail promises, and bruised ego and hips.
Tired of being unsure of the next second
when all I have ever been is second.   Or third.   Or ninth.

Does it matter what place
if I couldn't ever place
myself clearly in anyone's life?

But when I tasted you,
tea became coffee,
white became red,
and my body became yours to consume.

So uncork the bottle.
Pour us another drink.
Fill it to the brim.
Wipe my mouth with your thumb
marking my soul for salvation.
Kiss my stained lips after.

Baby, please say we are drinking the same.
I can't go back to Pinot after tasting Cabernet.
I see the way your hands hold your glass,
and I imagine how you could hold me forever,
but would you if you knew
I am far more
sharper and frailer
than these used cups?

Haunted

There are ghosts living in my head.
I will compare them to the way you will hold my hand.
The pretty words you will coo into my ear
have already been dissected syllable by syllable
before we even get the chance to meet.

My eyes will stare beyond yours
and into the past of lovers who dangled their love
like carrots molding in real-time, but I never kept up
to see the lies their eyes mirrored onto my smile.

The smile I should have saved for you.

Our hands will touch
and you still will not be able to feel me fully there.
You will know I am far away.
Lost in memories,
I remember to forget
why I should let myself be loved by you.

You will do your best to kiss the tears away
with promises to never make the same mistakes they did.
The ghosts will consider crossing over
this bridge you will try to build between us.

They will not.

And I will go further and further from you.

I will look for you from the other side
and wonder where we went wrong
before you arrive.

Can I Ask You Something?
First Published with Latino Book Review March 2021

Can I dive headfirst down your throat,
       or will you choke on all I am?

Can I backstroke through your bloodstream all the way to your heart,
       or will we always be slightly offbeat?

Can I curl up inside your stomach and spoon feed you my mother's recipes,
       or will you starve us of attention?

Can I dance in circles in your lungs and be swept up and down, in and out,
       or will I blow this up before it has a chance to breathe?

I can make myself home
in the creases of your dry elbows,
the knots in your upper back,
the pus ready to pop on the pimples you hate but I love,
in the swelling of your feet after a long day,
in your bit-down-to-the-cuticles nails that never scratch
when exploring my inner thoughts,
your abdomen folds folding right into mine after eating me up,
and in our knees bumping into each other as we try to sleep.

Can your body handle mine,
  or will it reject this donor's heart and transplant me somewhere else?

I don't care for the glitter
the gold
the picturesque poetry people want.

This body is meant

for
windows open, lights on, clothes off,
sweat and noises and hot breath

for
food stuck in between teeth,
overbites and understanding

for
you and you and you
and me.

Can you slip me on like your favorite pair of Docs,
or will you eventually wear me down
until I am nothing
but a pair of hands
holding onto a memory?

There's a Secret Message in This One

my favorite part of the nIght
is when you ask if i'll write about you

if i publish a million poems for you
will you read them

if i share stories of you
will you colLect them

the legend of you may outgrOw us
but will you still believe in me

become godlike for others
but stay deVoted to me

dedicate songs no other human can hear
and curatE your life around me

worship you with art and stanzas
but don't run off like run-on sentences

write letters all over you
but don't picture your life without me

stay in the sYllables wrapping around us
wrapping around each other

nothing in between you and me
except shared memOries

if i write about you
will i stay your favoUrite past this night

Jupiter

when my Jupiter was in detriment,
yours came in strong to keep me in your gravity

I orbited around your eyes
your laugh, an earthquake to the core

my Sun and Moon had no place to call home
your Jupiter called to them

Mercury, always in retrograde
Mars, always in war

Venus was alone
searching for a love after her house was broken
by rulers who placed their planet firmly
into her chart without permission

your Jupiter was a balance
my Venus needed

across fixed lines and square offs
my fire did not burn your earth
your earth did not stifle my fire

we navigated stars and planets
rose and fell
to create new constellations
only we could explore

Jupiter was never that far from Venus
space and time are nothing to two planets
crashing into each other

so we crashed and
Boom!

landed in the middle of my living room

The Answer

Every swipe right was a wrong turn.
Every pick up line was a let me down.
Repeating patterns orchestrated by loneliness and hope.
Those two lovers wouldn't leave me alone.

Found my way down too many glasses,
over poured and under delivered.
Still, I drank as if love would come from my liver.

Flooded in memories,
and drunk on cocktail tears,
I looked through the emptiness
filling out all the broken hearts here.

Saw you before you saw me.

And broken patterns replaced broken promises,
with orchestrated playlists *tamed* and *swift*.
Those two lovers just wouldn't leave us alone.

Every left swipe was a right turn.
Every down on my luck has brought me up
to dancing in living rooms when all the bars were closed.
Dreaming of everything we are, of everything we will be.

Loved me before I loved me.

And there on a couch in a bar, I met you.
And there on a couch in a house, you loved me.
And there on a couch, it was asked.

And those two lovers?
They finally left.

You Forgot Something

I awoke one rainy morning with a piercing pain in my chest.
I went under my nightshirt and felt
                                        nothing.

My skin and muscles and bones had gone in the middle of the night,
                        left my heart exposed.

I gently curled my fingers around its cries
and placed it on the kitchen counter.
It was still working,
beating like a newborn drum trying to find its rhythm.
With a kitchen knife,
                I sliced it
                    down
                    the
                    middle
                without thinking
            into two imperfect halves.
                        I took the right side
                        and it felt wrong alone
                    but I began to peel the layers
                    like an onion, or an orange,
                        or any fruit or vegetable
                        I had peeled before
                and fed His hunger while I starved.
                            I peeled
                        and I peeled
                    and nothing was wrong.
                No abnormalities, no nothing.
And so into the left I went.
I brought back the kitchen knife
and diced it into cubes.
Perhaps in this shape I could find what was wrong,
but it was still beating,
and I was still confused.

I left the cleanest mess on the counter.
No blood, no scars,
as if I was never there.

And if my cat ate my heart,
then let her.
Maybe she'll have more use for it.

Back in my room,
I slipped into my bed,
turned to one side,
faced the pastel pink wall,
and somehow fell asleep.

When I awoke again in the afternoon,
I turned to the other side of our bed
and you were not there.

You never were.

Somehow slipped away with my bones and muscles and skin,
                                          and left my heart behind.

Unholy

It's me.

You half-drunkenly whisper at 1:30 AM
and dangle me by a phone call
wooden and heavy
but I carry your baggage
like it is made of gold and salvation
blinded by my devotion
on the brink of starvation
with our nightly communion.

I swallow my pride more times
than I do you.
Begging on my hands and knees
for you to want me too.
Attend your church every night
and nail myself to your bedposts.
And every morning
I leave less holy and more ghost.

Love Bombs

When the fireworks stopped
When the passion ceased
When the you with me went dark again
I looked around

When the morning arrived
When the words had been laid down
When the lone soldier had departed
I saw this for what it was

The bed in disarray
The soldier's rifle left
The wounds not healed

The string you led me on
a fuse to a bomb ready to go off

Everything disintegrated
You disinterested
I disoriented

When the bombing began
the false start exploded

When the bombing continued
the war was not at all fair

When the bombing ended
the love never began

You Said You Didn't Want to be a Father

We swore we would never become our parents
but here we are.

You became your father
and I became your mother.

Chewing me out loudly.
Teaching my mouth to stay closed.

You became your father
and I became my mom.

Promises with no follow-through.
Follow-through with no promises.

You became your father
and I became my dad.

Leaving and coming back.
Dead with no hope of returning.

A Funeral of One

The first time you came back,
I bought a shovel.

Dug a hole 6 feet down
and buried the last amount of respect
I had for myself.
Hosted the funeral,
left no tear dry with the eulogy,
and adorned the church
with all the flowers
fresh as newfound love.
The casket, a red mahogany.
The body, still breathing.
The lover?
      You did not attend.
But there my respect and I laid
in that graveyard bed,
decaying under grass
and 6 layers of dirt
and memories.

And then
because this is California,
an earthquake broke open the ground,
and banged on my coffin.
Like electric cables jump starting my broken down love,
it sent shockwaves through the after-thought I had become.
The carcass that was my heart
was reminded that I once was alive to feel something.   *Anything.*
And the maggots slithering in and out
all through a large cavity that kept rotting away,
stopped dead in their tracks.
There was a smell now.
But my chest up and down somehow
made me think I could breathe now.

The earth had split open
and the sunlight reached her hand down
to scream *Now!*

I crawled on elbows through 6 feet of memories.
Dug my hands into 6 feet of dirt
and clawed my way up
                and up
                    and up
                      until
                            I felt that fresh air reach my lungs.

You were not there.
You had come back only when I was quiet.
But the moment the dirt shook,
you knew this was no earthquake.

It was your old lover rising from this grave
and I would not *shut the fuck up* anymore,
so your silence
would no longer be louder
than my heart beating
                    beating
                          beating.

I was beating myself
to save you.
But in losing you,
I have no use for a shovel now.
And if you ever choose to come back again,
know that there is no need for an aftershock
to remind me of my worth.

I will not bury myself again
and place you on top
with dead flowers
and a cracked tombstone that reads:

                Here lies One.
          She gave and she gave
to a boy who never offered to take the shovel
              and let her rest.

Act II: The Rising

The Kiss

At least Judas kissed Jesus
before he sent him to his death.

I can't remembered if you did
when you fucked me over

or even just fucked me.

Gaslighter

I burn up in my sleep while you are sleeping,
                                      you complain.
                                              I am sorry.
I turn the AC on, but that does not cool fast enough,
                                        you complain.
                                              I am sorry.
I rid our bed of blankets, but I am still burning up,
                                      you complain.
                                             I am sorry.
I feel the flames flick,
                    flick,
                          flickering on my skin.
                                  Reality no longer fits.
                        I was so sure.
          Am I sure?

When did I bathe myself in gasoline?   *Don't you remember?*
When did I strike the match?   *Don't you remember?*
When did I burn my world into ashes trying to light up yours?
                                            Don't you remember?

I don't remember.
        I don't.
             The flames at home in and out of my pores.
                                The sweat covering us both.
             The temperature keeps rising.
                          I can't breathe.
             You pour the fuel.
                                        I was so sure.
                                            I was.
                                  I am.
                        You are?
                I don't know.
            I don't know.
       Why is it so hot?
Stop it.
                       Stop it!
                             Combustion feels close.
You feel so far.
                                       I was so sure.
I am.
                  You are?
                                    Sorry.

Adams

When was the last time
my splintered soul did not attract a man
trying to cum all over my broken parts
and glue them back together?

It doesn't ever dry quick enough for them.

Would You Like a Refill?

The First took the glass of water I had barely poured
for myself
and found the taste too salty.
Drank it until his lips chapped
and then said no more.
He then pretended like the glass had never been poured at all
and laughed about his way
with other party guests in tow
at the parties I threw
for myself.

The Second drank.
And drank.
I bought a pitcher.
I bought gallons.
I bought a whole watering truck
and still he asked for more.
I was always thirsty, but so was he.
So I poured
and poured
and poured
and the glass was never full for him.
Eventually he left,
but not before smashing several glasses
and demanding I walk through them
to serve him one last drink.

The others after him,
I served vodka in water bottles.
I forget the number.
I forget the names.
I forget who I was during those times.

The Third never touched the glass.
He watched it be filled to the brim,
overflow onto the table,
and warp the foundation of us.
Once in a while, he would dip his fingers
to see if the temperature was to his liking,

and I would pour some more if he smiled.
But he did not drink.
The room filled to the ceiling and
I don't know to this day how he did it,
but he left the room without flooding the rest of the house.
Even when he was gone,
I still kept pouring.

The Last was a combination of all 3 before Him.

The drink was too salty.
The drink never satisfied.
The drink could go untouched for as long as he pleased.

The floor
still not dry from the last,
still stained with blood and glass from the one before,
still covered in confetti from all the parties in the beginning.

And I was still pouring,
but no longer water,
for the source had run dry.

The Twist Everyone Saw Coming

But I didn't.

Until his phone lit up.
And then,

my whole world went dark,
our love lost signal,

and hell hath no fury
like a poet scorned.

Every Love Story Needs a Fuck You Poem

How many did it take for you to feel any guilt?
How many did it take to get you to feel anything at all?

Did these girls' manicured hands around your neck
break your windpipe
that you couldn't breathe long enough
to get some oxygen to your head
and remember us / me?
Did their fingers snap your vocal chords
so you couldn't say my name
as they whispered yours through the phone?

Did their freshly done feet coil around you
and nail you to the ground
that you couldn't move?
Did you struggle to remember us / me
so much, you could only focus on
how it would feel to nail them?

Did all their photos
amount to the reality standing before you?
Did all their replies
push all my unread "I love you's" out of your heart?
Did all the money you spent on them
make up for how stingy you were with your love with me?

How many would it take to reach good enough for you?
How many would you introduce to your family and friends?
How many would you care got home safely after?

Or did you line up nine after another
once I had kissed you goodbye?

Why won't you answer me?
Don't answer that.

But how many did it take for ME to break free of you?

One.

My Hope in Your Sins

I hope each one of those girls
made you feel like a man,
a cheap thrill dressed in stilettos you paid for.
Made you feel wanted, needed, and loved,
all the things you never had me feeling with you.

I hope she gave you fuck me daddy eyes
while you worked with her during the day;
and when you had sex with me that night,
I hope you thought of her
because I wasn't thinking of you.

I hope you kept thinking of them
when you cooked my heart,
served me to the rats,
and smirked across the dinner table.

I hope their photos were worth it
because I can't ever picture us together again.

I hope the heels you bought for them to parade in were worth it
because I will never tiptoe on broken glass to only be an option
to you.

I hope their touch was worth it
because you will never touch me again.

I hope the months of lying created a truth you can lie in
because you are done laying next to me.

I hope the emptiness inside of you is finally filled
because I am done pouring my love into you.

Did You Really Just Ask Me That?

I am the whole table,
the chairs, the kitchen, the five star menu.
I am the bites you take.
The pride you should have swallowed.
I am the nutrition your body lacks.
The calcium for your bones.
The oxygen to that brain of yours,
inhaled through that mouth of yours
that has the audacity to ask me
what do I bring to the table.

What did you bring to the table?

The table you made a mess on.
The table I should have walked away from.
The table we dined in candlelight glow.

No dishes, only shit.
Cracked glasses, no plates.
Secret guests, zero reservations.

If only you had cooked
as good as you lied.

So I ask you again:
What do you bring to the table?

Magdalena

I wash my body raw,
hold scraps of flesh
in palms anointed with blood.

No matter how hard I try
I attract those who keep leaving marks
on a body that I pray God will unbless

until one goddamn day
I am not the only one repulsed by the image in his eyes.

But no matter how many scars I leave,
he keeps coming
and I keep taking burning showers,
hoping I no longer feel his hands clawing past my body
and ripping my soul into shreds.

Can I Ask You Something?
(Reprised)

I dove down my throat
                                       when you choked on your lies.
I felt my blood run cold
                                       when your attention ran off.
I went to the pits of my stomach
                                       when my heart dropped into its trenches.
I swam up my esophagus one-handed
                                       when my lungs gasped for air.

                           You made yourself home
                           in the creases of my eyelids,
                           the knots in my dyed hair,
                 the pussy you loved and the ass propped up,
             in the swelling of my breasts after a long period,
in my chipped nail polish after my anxieties scratched my outer flaws,
      my stretch marks stretching over you after you ate me up,
   and in our knees bumping into each other as we tried to sleep.

Did all those girls get naked like me
                                   or did they just take off their clothes?

                      You only cared for the glitter
                              the gold
                      the pictures you paid for.

                     This body was not meant
for   for
closed doors, told off, cheated on   being stuck in between others
tears and screams and cold words   overshadowing and underhandedness

                            for
                 you and you and you
                    and lastly, me.

I will slip you on like my favorite pair of hoops,
                                         and eventually wear you out
until you are nothing
                   but a pair of feet
                              that never stayed to make a memory.

Character Development

You: *hearts stuck together like book pages*
Me: *drenched in salt tears and french kisses*
You: *hands printing words on skin*
Me: *plot twists and characters on the side*

        maybe if you had focused on developing your character
              this scene would not need so much rehearsal

                      don't get me wrong
                      you almost had me
                believing I wasn't meeting
              your sky high expectations
               had me playing all the roles
              that weren't enough for you
            I even started to typecast myself

             but recently I've had a revelation
                call it character development

where the scene partner does not dictate my line
where the director has not placed himself in the lead role
where the stage manager does care about the actors' safety

              I am not the ingénue I once was
            and you were never a leading man
          we played these roles as best as we could
               and blamed it on the script
only to later realize we were improvising the whole thing

                  it was all a play to you
               and while I am an actress
              I try not to act in real-life
           you saw the lights and camera
       and called action with all of your inaction
              so I did what I do best

                      and cried on cue

In The Garden

If I am so toxic,
let me be the poison that kills all the snakes
(I mean boys)
who spit venom into my mouth
and called it making love.

If I am so ungrateful,
maybe it was all the shit you tried to feed me,
but my body knew better
and rejected it.

If I am a wilting rose,
oh God, please put me out of my misery!
Pull me from the root
and burn the soil,
so nothing ever grows here again.
Spare your hands the dirt in the nails
trying to revive me.

Let me die
if I have become
this toxic,
this ungrateful,
this wilting rose.

Put an end to my love
worming its way into you,
and planting seeds inside the deepest secrets you hold.
They sprout out of every hole you have.
Does that picture make you squirm?

Good.

I want— no I _need_
all my fruit to rot before it touches your lips.

If everything runs through me
and into us,
grab the hedge clippers,
the chainsaw,
whatever you want to use,
and end this.

Why try to save something
that will only die come the winter
covered in snow and paranoia?
Bury me now
and go watch the leaves change colors.
They burn bright with reds and yellows.
Never these blues you said I had too much of.

I swear there was a time when
my petals bloomed under your touch,
but I fell apart when you didn't think me
beautiful enough.
But I tried.
I did.
Thinking I could outsmart nature,
but you failed to ever nurture us.

So let me die
in this garden
where apples never grow,
snakes never tempt,
and Eve was always better off
                        without Adam.

Act III: The Climax

The Wind

I never wanted to be one of two ships
sailing past another
cursing the wind.

So you named me
the wind.

You a lone ship in still waters
with nowhere to go
until I came along.

                                     I wish I had sunk you instead.

Woman Like Me

Your dad will chastise you for dating a woman like me.
Your mom will advise you to grow up because I am a woman who knows
what she wants.
Your sister will sigh in disappointment, *if only she could have controlled
her emotions.*
Your other sister will be left untouched in this heartbreak warfare.
Your nieces will ask about me every chance they remember.
Their words, a reminder that a woman like me does not go forgotten.

But your aunt will threaten me to stay silent,
will bring my unborn child into this mess you gave birth to.
What if your child did the things you are doing?
But what if your child does the things you already did?

Your friends will call me a *bitch*.
The *crazy ex-girlfriend* trope, so original.
Others will have my back, and stab me in the front.
Others will believe me silently and never talk about you as loudly.
Many will form a wall and block any of my words from getting to you.
The *bros before hoes* trope, so misogynistic.

Your vices will be split in half.
Some will defend the money you sent them.
Some will provide receipts and send them to me.
Some will accept you with excess.
Some will deny you any more access.
All you made complicit in your actions.

Your world may crumble and fall apart.
Your world may stay together as I break down.
But you know what kind of woman I am
and the woman I am not.

I am not the silent victim.
I do not represent your past quiet slip-aways.
I am not the witch they burn at the stake.
I do not repeat my past, *don't make a fuss.*

I have learned to never let the reasons
they won't believe me, nothing will change
be the why's I burn myself at the stake before I even go to trial.

You know what kind of woman I am.

Your dad will warn you to stay away from a woman like me.
A witch who is not afraid to spell everything out for everyone.

Into the Flames

flick, flick, flickering
The emergency lights echo into the night.
click, click, clickering
My fingers spellbound to get this right.

You and your easy way outs.
You and your hardened soul.
I could not trust you to be honest
when your tongue would hiss why this ended.
I could not trust you to be honest
when their tongues would counter how this barely begun.

If you wanted to burn this bridge,
give me the matches.
I'll do it for you.

If you wanted to burn me down,
my words are the gasoline.
I'll press send on every message to all you know.

But be careful.

They cannot burn witches anymore.
Not when I hold the torch in my hands now.

They cannot hang witches anymore.
Not when they hang onto every word I curse now.

They cannot feed the flames as much anymore.
Not when they know I am an Aries Witch now.

She's a witch! She's a witch!
They cry
as they forward you all my messages.

I'm a witch! I'm a witch!
I set myself on fire
as I drag you into the light.

Orange

When the last ember died
When the last message was sent
When the last tear rolled down
I was covered in ashes

When I reached the end of words
When I unpacked the words of pain
When I mastered the pain of silence
I was released of tension

The fire crackled its goodbye
The future sparked no more
The Fates cut the bond

No more you and I
No more fire

The red dissipated
The yellow diluted
The orange…

I loved you in the orange
the in-between passion and light

I loved you in the orange
until there was no more

I loved you

Maneater

I gain weight by swallowing my pride,
but it's hard to keep it down
without a stiff drink
and a stiffer body.

So I stumble into the nearest bar
and out with the closest flesh.
Back alleys and back seats.
Lowlights and lower inhibitions.

My lips taste him
and then my mouth does.
Our teeth smash into each other,
like our hands are not enough to get a sense of who we are.
My legs wrap themselves around him
because my heart will never.
I count his breaths as they slow down and make no noise.
Shhh. There now.

Done, I walk home alone.

I struggle to spit out the aftertaste of his tongue.
Not enough saliva, too much teeth,
whereas mine are full of cavities
from gnawing on bones
trying to feast on any meat
in all their low carb, let's get high motives.
Oh and one root canal
from chewing a boy's arm off my throat.
I choked that whole summer.

I brush my teeth when I am home.
I find hair stuck in the back of my throat.
Blonde, brunette, no red heads
yet.
I gargle, rinse, repeat.

I forget to floss.

I kick off my heels.
His sweet, sticky warm crimson pulses
in between my toes.
Must have soaked through.

I'll shower in the morning.

My shoulder blades melt into the cool pillows
and my gut trembles.

Still hungry.

I drag my feet to the freezer
because for now,

leftovers. Again.
Left over. Again.

So tonight
which is it?

The gin? The vodka?
The Italian who played guitar in the fountain for me
once upon a time?
His heart was dessert drizzled in tequila.
It burned on the way down,
but provided me enough energy to dispose of him later on.
His head made the sweetest noise
as he laid his face in between my legs
and I swallowed him whole.

Or the German side dish that let me devour him
without question,
with as much gusto as he could tie me up?
I slipped out before he could realize he was tied up in me.
I miss him tonight.

So I open my jaw and take a bite.
He's cold now.
But there is no point in thawing a man
who had no need for a heart
when it came to me.

It's an eat or get eaten kind of world
and it is not my fault
I have such a sweet tooth
for spoiled sour men,
but even he has gone bad for my liking
tonight,
so I drink.

I gargle, rinse, repeat.

More hair comes out,
long, mine.
I am eating myself inside out
or is it outside in?

It's 12:45 AM
and I can make last call
to find another.

I grab my coat,
almost forget a new set of heels,
and lock the door on the way out.

It's true what they say.
You become what you eat.
And after feeding on scraps for so long,
I am still scraping the bottom of a stiff drink
and a stiffer body.

The Hook Up After the Break Up

Please keep me in between your teeth.
Grind me into what you want.

Have your hands search for foreign languages
when you believe I have visited new countries.
Rewrite me then
into a version they wish they could have fucked me into,
reclaiming pounds of flesh they should have never conquered.

Etch braille onto my ass that only your taste buds can read.
I stopped reading in your native tongue,
the one I could hear for weeks,
when you decided to no longer speak to me.
Your silence makes no difference to me now.

Fuck me into a memory.
Only to be remembered with your hand
when you get too lonely
and I no longer pick up your call.

Upon Entering

Did you find yourself
inside of me?
Did you find me?
If you did,
can you tell her
I've been looking for her?

She took a vacation
and never came back.
She took my favorite shirt
and smile.
Mumbled something about needing more milk,
even when we had 3 different flavors in the fridge.
She packed while I was sleeping,
kissed me goodnight,
promised she'd be right back,
but it's been over a lifetime ago.

The very milk she promised she'd buy
is now sitting in the kitchen
covered in missing ads.
I think it's her.
I can't recall her face.

Did she leave because I dunked all my Oreos and spoiled the taste?
Did she become lactose intolerant because I couldn't tolerate her at times?

I said I was *sorry*.

I promised to be on my best behavior,
but I guess what was best for me
wasn't for her.

Did she run to a big city and get lost on her way back?
Or did the open road call to her and now my calls keep going to voicemail?

*Please pick up. It's so lonely here without you.
I don't know who I am without you.*

What did you find when you entered me?
What made you run away so fast when you exited?
Did you come across the real you?
The real me?

Tell her to come back
if you find me in someone else.

I've Read This Somewhere Before

Are we David and Goliath?
One for the downfall,
the other for glory.

Or Daniel and the Lions?
Everyone terrified for us,
but we speak in languages
only we understand.
And when they find us,
they find themselves
bewildered we did not eat each other alive.

Don't let us be Jonah and the Whale.
I swallow you,
but now you're inside of me,
and I'm afraid of what you will find.
Or worse,
you swallow me
and I'm now a part of you
until you throw me out.
But I have your stench all over the better of me.

Gardens in Babylon
grew thorns from gardeners
who could not communicate.
But the problem with us
is not our tongues moving
in synchrony,
but that they do not speak
what we wish would grow
between us
and decay surrounds us instead.

And before you know it
we find ourselves locked in towers
we pay for in secret hotel visits
and Babel our way through with each other
because we are just two kids
who fell in love
as adults playing house.
My God,
why did we play house so well?
Characters we made up

and now I don't know what's real.

I would rewrite this tale if I could.
Take pen to paper,
burn old and new testaments
so no one can testify
against us.

I am in love with you
but love did not keep Abraham
from almost killing his son
when God ordered him to sacrifice his child.
Will you sacrifice me
when your inner child is yelling
for your father?
Will you become your father?
Will I become mine?

Take me back to the gardens
where we fell in love.
Take me back to the beginning
and let us rapture each other all over again.

Skipping Ahead

you were so keen to skip past accountability,
you would not face what you had left behind
if you had stopped looking at everyone else at the finish line,
you would have faced what you were really leaving behind

        my bed, our drives
        your morning coffee, my desserts
        orange roses, violet towels
        first dance, first screams
        head scratches, stomach pats
        long days, endless fights
        longer nights, dirty talks
        scrabble laughs, jenga dates
        slammed doors, drive-offs
        gray hairs, eyebrows plucked
        sweet kisses, bitter congratulations
        dishes cooked, dishes washed
        playlists shared, isolating silence
        shit-talking, talking shit
        football beers, rom-com wines
        my fears, your crimes
        one more kisses, *one more*, *one more*
        i love you, i love you too
        me, us

        we created a whole life in my heart,
        but you skipped ahead and left me behind

The Ending is Here

It came with a bang and the softest feather falling onto the couch.
It brought Malibu and Rosé.
It left a haunting at a crossroad to envision a possible sequel,
but no one likes a sequel quite like the original.

You were never an original,
and foolishly I still gave glowing reviews.

I drank the afterparty favors,
watered down by our tears.
You begged for another chance,
and I almost gave it to you.
Until the morning brought its epilogue
and there for all, more lies were hung to see.

And you...
                begged for another chance.
And I...
                almost gave it to you.

You were standing in the middle of my place,
and my hallway always looked good on you.
I played house so well
that you forgot to actually build a home for us.

Why am I still searching for a reason to give you another chance?

There was never going to be a housewarming.
Just us burning down.
A crash.
A land.

So I stopped reasoning with myself to search for another chance.

You begged
and I almost.

I almost.

Alternate

What if they had never died,
would Romeo still love Juliet?

What if I had never told our friends,
would it capitulate all our problems for you?
What if you had never done what you did,
would I still be on my balcony waiting for you?

What if we only remember that classic love story
because their story never experienced life?
What if their love was death-marked so young
because old love is not easy, but never dies?

What if they had listened to their households
both alike in worry?
What if they had never met with masks on
both alike in *sorry*?

What if I could stop everyone's grudges breaking into mutiny?
What if I could unlay the scene where everything went wrong?
What if I could uncross the stars?

What if I could rewrite their ending,
would it change ours?

What if I am actually Rosalind
never to be heard of again?

Before I Say Goodbye... Again

The second time you came back,
I no longer needed a shovel.
It seems I had lied on my previous deathbed.

The lights from the Christmas tree
shined upon the horrifying miracle
of this damned season.

You laid your head on my lap,
like I was your personal Santa Claus
ready to give you all that you wished for.

I died a second time
sitting there on that couch
I loved you for so many holidays before.

I no longer needed a shovel
because you would receive all my gifts this winter
regardless if I was dead or alive.

While with the coal you gave me,
I should have set you on fire
and kept myself warm for once.

But I was a hopeless romantic,
who believed if I loved enough
I could turn this coal into a diamond,

and you into a man who would love me
for the first time since we met.

Act IV: The Fallout

Genre

If this is a movie,
you are a tragedy.

If this is scripted,
I am a comedy.

But I never got the joke.
You never got the point.

Both watching two different reels,
unaware of the roles
we had been playing with each other.

Mothered

My mother held me as I fell apart once more.
Let me sleep in her bed for nights and days.
I couldn't breathe long enough
to believe I would wake up in the mornings to come.

How many tears can a mother dry up
until her shirt is soaked to the bones?
Bones begging to feel this pain
instead of her daughter.

So, she prayed:

*If all the shit you've been through didn't kill you,
if your father dying didn't kill you,
if you trying to kill yourself didn't kill you,*

*having one more person walk out of your life
will not be the end of you.*

*Cry it all out.
Do what you have to do to get through this.
But get through this.*

He will not be what kills you.

*You are strong
not because of the love you receive or don't.
You are strong
because of the love you are capable of giving
and you have so much left in you to give.*

Our Games
In 2 Parts

I. Scrabble
The words I had come to believe
were never my own.
I loved him so much,
I heard his voice coming from my own mouth.

His words split my tongue into two
to accommodate his hate.
Still, I could not call on myself to play
in fear I would be too much for anyone to love.

The words never scored triple,
but I doubled down on the love I felt
as I placed his things into 4 wooden crates,
unmarked, unlike me.

II. Jenga
The dreams I had for us scattered all over the floor.
A game of jenga is how I met him.
A game of jenga is how I am left.
A game of jenga is in one of those 4 wooden crates.

I had hoped he would have unstacked the mess he left in me
with the precise wording that could have scored him endless points.
I was not a prize, but I am human.
I fell too, when he was out of place.

The games we played.
The games he played.
The games I was played.
Now in 4 wooden crates.

I & II
I wanted to keep playing with him.
His laugh, forever on the board.
Our future plans, forever written on the blocks.
My hope in those 4 wooden crates
I returned to him.

Habits

Time heals all wounds,
but I had a habit of picking at scabs.
So I broke my habit
when you broke my heart.
Time did its healing.
No longer an open wound,
my heart picked new habits.

Stay

When I lay in bed, I cannot sleep
without my hand on my right hip bone.
It reminds me there's something under the rolls of flesh.

When a scar fully forms on my skin,
I scratch it until it bleeds.
I need to know there's still a heart working underneath this shell.

When my thighs rub together,
I pray to God no one else can hear the fabric ripping apart.
No. I don't need another pair of jeans.

When I'm pulling at my hair,
it's the tiny pricks on my head that remind me I am here.
I am not a figment of someone else's imagination
of who I dream to be.

Or maybe I'm hoping the more I pull,
the quicker I'll disappear.

When a loved one holds me in their arms,
I try to make myself smaller.
Hoping if my body is tiny,
then maybe so will my anxiety.

And

maybe if there's less to carry,
there will be less of a chance
of everyone I love
leaving me.

An Insomniac's Prayer

Lord help me
when the clouds turn into smoke,
when the rivers become blood,
a transformation short of a miracle.

Lord help me
when the tears over texts are twisted dry,
when the streets are emptied of souls,
a deserted nation with long ways to go.

Lord help me
when I awaken and my lover is gone,
when my body is still here, but I am done.
A warm bed, cold feet.
Forget washing them.
Cover them in blankets
once thrown to the ground.

Lord help me.
I've got dirt in between my toes
and in my fingernails.
Clawed my way out of my own dug grave to pray
Lord help me.

I've had no revelations.
Only raptured my body for those promising false salvation.
Lord help me.

The clouds have separated.
The rivers are still water.
The streets, full.
The texts, deleted.
And my love will not return for the third time.

Lord help me.
This heart is tired
and this love needs sleep.

Rain Room
Inspired by Random International's Rain Room

I drowned in an empty room.
Stood under a rainstorm
that never flooded
and never touched my skin.
Dehydrated and so close to dying,

I stood in an empty room.
A single light outlining my unforgotten body.
I did not know how to move without chasing
waterfalls and shadows of a former visitor.
Remembering of deaths long ago,

I prayed in an empty room.
Could see God's melancholy falling from the skies,
but never felt it reach my soul.
My lips could see forgiveness in the air.
With only memories of living,

I paced in an empty room
to the drips of artificial rain
caused by the realest pain.
Waiting for Death to visit
and quench a thirst I could not forget.

The Final Death

I learned the Living and the Dead should not mingle when my father died.
That grief had to be dealt with.
That heaven was not a place on earth.
That purgatory was not conducive for those who wanted to live again.

If this was a book,
this is where I'd kill your character off
and never write about you again.

But this is life.

And in life,
I had to actually kill the version of me
who would go on loving you.

I knew I would not survive in the what if's and should have's,
because memory is a deadly weapon
and it was killing any chance of me moving on.

And I could die
like I had died before and the time before that,
but I refused to become some sort of zombie,
dragging my feet across roads we once drove down.

And I was definitely not going to become a ghost,
haunting my own house when I began to miss you.
I could not be in possession of my own body
and still call it living.
Ghosts can scare the shit out of you,
but not life into a loss.

If I wanted to live past this death of us,
I had to permanently die along with it.

I took the memories out of my head.
I took the life I once held in my hand.
I took it all out in sweat and tears.
I took it all out.

This version of me
you had given a burning paradise to,
I took her out
and gave her the final rest
she desperately needed.

The Night the Devil and I Never Met

Because life would not stop for me,
I did for one night.
Felt my heartbeat come to a still,
and waited for Him to arrive.

I closed my eyes
speaking of the Devil,
so He would show up.
I spoke of you all through the night.

But what does it mean when you never did?

I could have sworn I never saw a miracle happen when you were around.
And God knows I prayed and prayed to make you a better man.
Our late-night confessionals turned blasphemous
as the holy light shined upon us.

Turns out, you were always just a boy.
I should have known.
My prayer had a name
and it was never yours.

In the morning and out of this slumber,
I detangled the cobwebs of a coffin no longer there.
I tasted the air, its fresh forgiveness.
I knew I would live today,
as I had the other days.

Life would not stop,
and neither would I.

Why God Made Women

One summer evening
when I was a questioning teen,
my devoted mother and I visited La Basilica in Mexico City.
As we entered the holy gates,
I noticed my fellow man
dragging their bodies across blessed pavement.
My eyes could not believe,
and I asked my mother,

"Why?"

She shared
the further they crawled on bare knees
to the cathedral
the stronger their prayer.
Their sacrifice matching their need.

"What why?"

Did they not know that man,
and prayer,
and gods,
are pointless one-sided communication?

"Like why?"

I spent my childhood knees stapled to the pews
praying to a god who never answered my prayers.
What makes God a god
when God has never been more than a bedtime story
my mother recited as we stood in front of a cathedral
one summer evening?

As we watched another man split his skin,
break bone and bread
to reach what I still believe to be four walls and no home,
my mother explained,

It is not God who they pray to,
but La Virgen.
This is Her church.

I stopped walking,
in disbelief and speechless.
My mother turned to me and asked,

"Why?"

Isn't it obvious?

"Like what?"

Man knows prayer to a god
will never reach him.
But begging a woman to pray on his behalf,
to fall onto her knees and raise her hands to the heavens,
only then will a god open his home because there is nothing more
than what a man-creating god loves
than a woman on her knees.

Ritual

as you peel back these layers of skin
preparing to crack open my chest
and analyze what keeps my heart ticking
all you will find is
all guts, no glory
for i have plucked my ribs two by two
to mold boys into men
12 pairs for every pair of hands
that deemed me their messiah

with a rib in each hand
they smacked them together
brought thunder to the earth
and armed themselves to pierce me through the heart

without my ribs
the path was clear for them to see
what was my heart
they fell to their knees
and chanted

El Corazón Sagrado. El Corazón Sagrado. El Corazón Sagrado.

these so-called disciples
prayed the rosary
burnt through the sage
danced themselves into a fervor
took the remaining part of me onto an alter
and left flesh to rot
as they held a rib in each hand
to see who had the biggest piece of me
who was worthy of taking this ticking heart too
this body was of no use they came to the conclusion,
but the heart
the sacred heart

is this how i could love so unconditionally
this heart of my bleeding with no ribs to protect
i laughed / they trembled

it's because my venus is in pisces
i mean it's because
my value is only worthy in pieces

they chanted all through the night
and when daylight broke on my back
they saw i was simply a woman in need of love too

but no one wants to believe their god is human too,
has needs too,
needs love too

and they took each rib as a stepping stone
became better men
and left me to sew these layers back up
had me apologizing
like i didn't mean to expose myself like this
i'm sorry

as they gathered themselves
i asked

will the next woman be there hallelujah
will they cry and say they're saved

i don't know but

stay away, stay away
i only want the living and fully formed with me

with you around
i forget who actually is the ghost

but wait
before you go

i want my ribs back

Act V: The End

And on the Third Day...

I had to shed skin faster than a snake.
I was Adam's remaining ribs
and the forbidden fruit not plucked off a dying tree.
I killed myself over and over and over,
but there was nothing biblical in my rebirth.
I was baptized in smoke.
Made angels in the ashes
of a garden that never grew anything,
except thorn-pricked ideas of love.
Their roses were always conditional to the touch.
I could not keep not wearing gloves
and bleeding all over my house.
I just couldn't.

So like my baby teeth falling out
and lovers walking away,
I learned bodies could be replaced.
And when my reputation no longer matched my reflection,
I knew what I had to do.
One always has to go.
It died and was buried.
The local choir sang at its funeral.
And somehow simultaneously,

I arose.

Daydreamer

I dreamt of love for so long,
I kept it imaginary.

Kept it in the movies,   melancholy.
In the books,   mythical.
In crisis,   messy.

I dreamt of love for so long,
but love never dreamt of me.

Kept me in the mundane,   denied.
In the bars,   drunk.
In chaos   desperate.

I wanted nothing more than to show love,

                                                                    Me!
                                                               Pick me!

But love wanted everything more than me,

                                                              Not me!
                                                You won't get me!

I dreamt of love for so long,
I forgot what love looked like   awake.

Alarms

For when you feel like picking up the phone,
call yourself to the document you created
where the pain could speak.

For when the pain calls to you,
pick up the document you printed
where you shared all you never spoke.

This document is bleeding truth
for you to never bleed again
from what he did to you.

28 + 25 pages,
single spaced, 12-point font, Times New Roman.
A thesis, an alarm.

Do not run back to the dagger
who had you write that document in blood.
Do not run back to the muse
who had you write this book in tears.

Set an alarm for each time he manipulated you.
Set an alarm for each time you cried
Why did you come back? Why me? and silence answered.
Set an alarm for each time your future asked
What if your child was with someone like him?
Set an alarm for each time you forgot your power.

Set the alarms.

Do not fall asleep on who you are
ever again.

Peach Cobbler

I used to bake
back when I had enough of me to spare.

I'd grab the flour to start.
Followed by too many cups of sugar
and a pinch of salt
for balance.
Then another pinch
of myself.
I'd keep pinching myself
until I felt something.   *Anything.*

Next,
I'd combine the ingredients.
Added enough water to keep me alive.
Stirred in the baking powder to prop me back up.
I'd debate about baking soda
unless the recipe called for it.
I was always out
and this had to get done.
Cracked an egg or two.
Then cracked myself a bit, or too
much for anyone to bother sticking
around to clean the mess.
So I'd drop in another stick of butter
to better myself.

But,
I'd always forget to preheat the oven,
too focused on the peaches and cinnamon.
Firm, but not too firm, or I'd scare him away.
Spicy, but not too much spice, or I'd leave a bad taste.

If preheating really was important,
then how was foreplay never an ingredient?

If he wanted me warm and ready,
he could have turned the dial to 350
instead of stuffing the dish inside.

If he really wanted to enjoy the peach cobbler
I spent hours making perfect for him,
he could have helped in the kitchen too.
Rolled up his sleeves and used those fingers of his
to finish the dessert he was always begging for.

Instead he did a 180,
and left me with no appetite for peach cobbler again.

For When They Try To Feed Bullshit

Why are you trying
to bring some store bought apple pie
and lie you baked it yourself?

I can smell rotten cores from a mile away.

To Never Being Certain

I don't hate you.
Not anymore.
                                    But know,
                        to have hated you meant
                        I loved you in the first place.

            I still love you in last place.

There's a stillness in my heart.
                    A peace that was never ours to promise.
                    A poem I could have written and rewritten.
            A home you could have slipped your hand into forever.

            Love is the only tenant in my house now.

There's an answer in my soul.
                                    If I were to once more
                            live this story with uncertainty,
                    the unknown does not frighten me anymore.

            You do not frighten me anymore.

There's a certainty in my bones.
                                    With certainty,
                            I can share with you
                            nothing in life is certain.

                Every person is a risk.
                Every choice is a life missed.
                Every ending is a beginning.

        There will always be an uncertainty in certainty,
            but there will no longer be a you in me.

Just a List of Things I Did

Consulted my astrologer. Duh.
Consulted a psychic. They're different.
Therapy. Lots of it.
Worked out. Too much of it.
No alcohol. Oh God, why!
No sad poetry.
No poetry = No sad.
Only women singing better off alone anthems.
Thought of those women. Thought of you.

Stop it.
Don't you cry.
Not at the grocery store.
Not in the produce aisle.
Come on!

Breathe.

Visited my dad. Didn't say much.
Talked with my mom. Shared too much.
Held my sister's hand. Really tight.
Called my friends. Too many times.
Got high once. Okay twice.
One date. None after that.
Masturbated.
Thought of you. Thought of me.

Wait. Stop.
Oh come on!
Not during this!
I just stopped crying!

Try again.

Stalked your social media. Stopped.
Deleted old photos. This took a while.
Gave away the four items I kept.
Forgot your phone number. Finally.
Read your horoscope. One last time.
Laughed at the thought of you reading my horoscope.
Thought of me.

Oh shit not again.
Oh shit. Not again?
No more tears!

Thought of me. Thought of me. Thought of me. Thought of me.
Let you go.

Today

Tomorrow, tomorrow
We'll do it tomorrow
you promised everyday
and the next day.

But when today came without you,
I went to the waters,
felt the earth beneath my sorrow,
and met Today.

Today will do for tomorrow,
and today I am standing
in the same spot where I sat with you
and Yesterday.

Today I am standing.
I am standing with Today
and tomorrow, tomorrow
I will stand with Tomorrow.

Viole(n)t

> "These violent delights have violent ends."
> - Romeo & Juliet, Act II, scene vi

In all the shades I have loved
from his orange to our blue,
love was always painted in such violent colors.

Sweet hues until the "I love you's" ran dry.
I learned to mold my heart into new shapes
in hopes I could keep drawing their attention.

But delight has an end,
and an end is no delight.

Unsaturated and unloved,
I took to my heart to see where we went wrong.
There in the mix of the arteries and veins,
the purples began to bleed together.

A new tint I had not dipped in,
but a stain my heart hoped would not wash off so easily.

In this violet glow,
I could see all the pathways to my heart.
The pigmentation iridescent,
the undertone not so under it cut with its tone.

I blushed looking at my own heart.

If loving myself this much
has a violent end,
let me rejoice in the delight
that is finally loving myself.

Let me viole(n)tly love myself
in all of my colors.

Let this love cast over me.
Let this love love me.

What Will I Do When This Book is Done?

I once wrote Boy into my life and loved him so much,
I thought I could change his mind.
"All I've ever wanted was for you to choose me."

I once wrote a poem about all I imagined us to be
and read it to him with the lines,
"Do you see us finding our love again?
I'm so afraid you'll never feel all my love."

I once wrote this book about our love story
and sent it to him with the hope,
"You still have time to change the ending."

I once put off the ending to this book for as long as I could,
as if time would rewind.
"I don't want to let him go just yet."

I once believed this book would not be about him,
until that night he called,
"I missed you. Did you miss me?"

I once believed he'd come back
and this book's ending would change.
I waited. He came back.
The ending did not change.

"I really did love you."
I don't know what I will do when I am done with this book.

I know there will be more to this story,
and subsequently,
this love.

I just don't know what that is yet,
but I'll make sure to write about it.

Bathroom Stall Lesson
a thank you to my friends

Do you remember when
you found me crying in that bathroom stall?
Held my hair back
as my world came crashing down.
Removed eyelashes barely hanging on
as I held onto you.

You, in your best dress and wisdom,
sat down on the beer-stained floors
and proclaimed,

"Boys like shiny things too,
but all the flashing lights make them go blind.
Let him wander through overpriced drinks
and no value moments.
All that shines, shines
until it doesn't."

Well, we lost our shimmer long ago,
but I still reflect the best in you.
Your earrings I wear now
whisper, "I have your back,"
and keep my head up.

The ring on my finger never rusts
as I wipe away any tears
that once would have worn me down.

When he never thought of me,
you gave me peace of mind
without a second thought.

When he tried to buy love elsewhere,
you gave me the change I sought
without a second to spare.

In you,
I find a friend.

In you,
I find love-stained memories
of nights on bathroom stall floors.
And I remember how
you pulled me up
and kissed the ring on my finger.
Our laughs vibrated throughout that whole night,
and I knew I would never not shine
with you by my side.

When All Was Lost

I found strength
in my mother's tears
as she sat at the edge of her bed
and I at the edge of life overlooking a cliff
I had been wanting to dive off for years.

I found worth
in my sister's slammed doors
and frustrated pleas
to stop abusing my heart
on behalf of an abuser who had never opened his door.

I found kindness
in my friends'
phone calls, texts, postcards, FaceTime,
ringing through the inner self doubt
ringing in between my ears.

I found a *give no fucks* confidence
in my cousin
as we danced around the living room
high off what life could offer
and edibles.

I found forgiveness in
the steps I took into renovated and desolate rooms,
the breaths that took up space in my own body,
the smiles I forgot my mouth could stretch into,
and the stretches my heart remembers long before it shrunk itself
for another.

I found love
out in the world
when I learned to love
the world in me.

A Love Only The Gods Can Hear
First Performed with Project LaFemme March 2020

This is for
the women who have swallowed more than they could stomach;
the ones that kept it buried so deep,
they almost forgot they could swim;
the woman who stayed, and the ones who left,
and the ones who are still going.

We bury so much, we bring our own shovels
and flowers to our own funerals, because,
"No, I don't want to bother you. I'm great. I can do this."
Smiles are easier than the truth.

We lie.
I lied.

For too long that I forgot I had cut out my tongue
and served it on a golden platter.
Held my breath in case my need for air was too loud.

Inhale, exhale, quietly.

Do not disturb the Dead and definitely do not wake up the Living.
Held my heart too close to my chest,
that it buried itself so deeply, it came out the other side
and left a hole in its place.

I tried to find it once.
Wandered through rooms, arms reaching out,
but slaps on the wrists or
my body pushed up against the wall
were the only things there to greet me.

I never knew what would happen if I spoke too much
or not enough.

When we, girl, are hurting,
we do not let depression make any noise.
Anxiety does not have a name,
and if it did, it definitely did not sound like ours.
When the cuts and bruises show, we bring out our makeup brushes
and glow that shit up.
Cover it all in bronzer, and eyeshadows, and wipe off the mascara tears.

When I, mujer, was losing my grip on who I was,
I swallowed my pride,
filled my stomach, overflowed to my throat,
and I choked on my own blood.
I had no tongue to stop it.
Still left on that golden platter.
Dried up blood on the corners of my smile.

When they said I was too much,
I learned to quiet my body.
It croaked dead on the spot
whenever I walked through the doors of any room too big,
and somehow I was still not small enough.

I learned to never ask for help.
That's fine. I know. I am strong enough.

When we, ladies, love, we love loudly.
Pronounce your name on an octave only the gods can hear,
caress every consonant,
and sing every syllable.

Your body was a dance floor,
and I knew all the moves to light it up.
Your lips were a deity I would sacrifice myself to worship.
I gave my heart and my body and my soul.

But when you said I was too much,
I had already learned how to be so quiet,
the Dead thought I was one of them.

Inhale, exhale, quietly.
Inhale, exhale.

How much more quiet could I get?

Was my own body willing to at least love me in the dead of night?
Make some noise for me?

I'd touched myself to see if my body would still react.
It did. I hated myself more.

I unlearned my name.
Burnt off my fingertips, so I could not feel my skin.
Walked away from my tongue on that golden platter.
I would go without tasting myself for years.

But can I ask?

Why must I quiet my love when you cannot find a reason to love me?
Why must I quiet my love when you cannot love yourself?

My love was once loud.
My body was a popstar winning grammys.
My heart was a drum that couldn't keep rhythm,
but that's okay because I never asked you to play with it.

Why must I stay quiet?

I am the banshee that will wail until the neighbors get called.
I am the witch who will cast love spells and hexes
in the same breath, under the same moon.
I am the bitch you will tell all your friends I was crazy.
God she was such a crazy bitch.
But I would rather be *a* bitch than *your* bitch.
I am a cunt, because that's what I become when you run out of words
to spit into my face.
I am the one you thought would wait a century and a half

while you made up your mind.
I am the wall you put your fist through.
I am the half-excused pat on my back when I had an anxiety attack
in front of you.
Asking me, "Are you done?" and then saying , "You need to go now."
I am the excuse you made up to break up with me
when you were too insecure of a boy.
I am the girl who sparked something in you
and the shit was too bright, so you finally saw your own reflection.
Guess you didn't like what you saw.

Do you think for one second I'd sit around
and wait for you to decide?
I am not the ocean tide,
and you are not a god to pull me back and forth like I am yours to own.

I am not going to sit around.
I won't be here waiting in the quiet of a love only gods can hear.

I am loud and I am soft.
I am so many things you will never experience
because you were looking for something better,
something quieter, something not too much.

Baby, we are always looking for something better...

But don't worry.

I am the heartbroken niña crying into ice cream
and a bottle of wine every Friday night.
I am "give me a few weeks and I'll be okay" out drinking with her
friends, out remembering why I thank the heavens my heart was broken
over and over again by boys pretending to be men.

Because when the pieces come back,
they come back in shapes I'd never be able to piece together
if you had decided you'd settle down with me shutting up.

I am not settling down for me shutting up.

Because

I'm over writing poetry for men
and their neediness to keep fucking
over this body with their so-called needs.
I'm through writing rhymes for women
who had me holding my breath
because maybe this would be the time
they would let me call them mine.
And I'm no longer apologizing for how I love
the fierceness in my bites,
the tenderness in my holds,
the I'm too sensitive for this shit
but let's pretend I'm the toughest bitch
you've ever fucked.
I'm not.
I'm not...
I'm not apologizing.
I cry and I laugh and I create art
with fingertips that will leave scratches down your back
and trace your lips when they curl up into a smile.
I want to know why you smile when you look at me?
Am I the prey you've been hunting?
Or am I a predator you think you can tame?

I am neither.

I am a goddamn mujer, who loves,
and I will love loudly.

Private Paradise

when the whole world has gone to sleep, i sneak away for a second to sit in the silence
of my car and watch the other drivers off to work at this hour.
it is not morning, but it is not night.
i wonder who else is awake. i sometimes wonder if you are.
this is the only time my head does not swim in words.
the only time i can think without thinking.
my heart does not ache. my eyes do not search the shadows of the past
and the future does not even cross my mind.
this is the only moment when i am truly present.
i never knew peace and i could be lovers.
i always feared that those who promised such things were con artists
and i was desperate enough to want it
that i would don the rose-colored glasses
and con my own heart.
i don't feel that desperation anymore. it left a while ago and i never said goodbye.
perhaps for the best, because i never understood the good in goodbyes.
no one comes knocking nowadays. the door is not locked,
but it is not inviting either.
where i live now is where i live now.
i have no visitors to attend.
i have given no one my new address.
i threw my phone into the lake
and never went back to see if it came to shore.
it is quiet here.
my heart once in a while looks out the window
when she hears our new neighbors laugh.
she still is a curious one, i'll give her that.
but it is quiet here.
it is home here.
and i don't think i'll be moving anytime soon.
so, let where i am now be the one thing i don't write about.
i have shared everything else, yes because i wanted to,
but because i had to as well.
it was getting lonely being surrounded by everything i had ever known.
i had to run away and i hope you can understand that. i do miss you,
but let this new home just be mine.

i promise to visit when i can.

love always,
J

Epilogue

The greatest love poem
I have ever written
is about falling in love
with myself.

(there is no ending to this one)

Acknowledgments

To my mom:
Everything I know about love, I learned from you.
Thank you for being my best friend.

To Kathy:
You are the very definition of love.
Thank you for being my soulmate.

To my dad:
This, and everything I do, is for you.
Thank you for keeping me safe from above.

To my brothers, Kevin & Jose:
A bit of tough love and a whole lot of hugs from you two.
Thank you for stepping up when I was knocked down.

To Tía Nilo & Tío Tony:
Thank you for being my home away from home.

To Tonya:
Thank you for your words. Thank you for your heart.
Thank you for being you.

To my therapist:
Thank you. Thank you. Thank you.

To Amahri, Charles, Danielle, Elizabeth, Juan, Laura, Marya, Peyton, Steph, Stephanie, Suki:
A person is only as strong as those who lift her.
Thank you for lifting me through the end of this story.

To Erin:
Thank you for kicking my heart and ass into shape.

To Alexandra:
Thank you for illustrating my version of a love album.

To the Tuesdays at CLI:
Thank you for giving me my mentors, my peers, and my friends.

To you:
May you love like tomorrow is not promised.
May you love like yesterday was a blessing.
May you love like today loves you because it does.
I swear it does.

Thank you for going on this journey with me.
I love you.

About the Author

Janette Valenzo

Janette Valenzo is a hopeless romantic.

She is also a bilingual queer Chicana poet, a teaching artist, an actor, and a mental health advocate based in Southern California. She's been published with Alegria Publishing, Los Angeles Poet Society Press, Dryland Literary Journal L.A., Hombre Lobo, and Latino Book Review. She has shared personal essays on mental health, along with resources she has compiled for BIPOC and LGBTQ+ communities, with More Love and Narratives of Hope. Her acting and spoken word has taken her to various stages throughout the country.

She currently teaches workshops with Arts Connection, Art With Impact, Story Pirates, and UCLA. Before working as a freelance teaching artist, she worked as an advance associate for the Obama Administration.

She reads Tarot cards and is an avid learner of astrology. She writes a monthly career Tarotscopes column with Powerful Latinas Rising.

She currently attends the University of Southern California for a Master of Education in School Counseling. She holds a Bachelor in Fine Arts in Drama from New York University's Tisch School of the Arts, where she studied at the Stella Adler Studio of Acting and Playwrights Horizons Theater School. She minored in Applied Theatre and Latin American Studies.

When she's not watching the latest Marvel series, she's in a getaway car. She's a Swiftie who really enjoys getting lost.

For more on her work, visit www.janettevalenzo.com.

www.ingramcontent.com/pod-product-compliance
Lightning Source LLC
Chambersburg PA
CBHW072206100526
44589CB00015B/2385